D1383487

START UGLY

A Timeless Tale About Innovation and Change

by Chris Krimitsos

The Perfect Execution

Dedicated to Steve Tingiris of Dabble Lab, who first planted the seeds for this story to take root and always helps me understand the nature of innovation and change.

Thanks to Lorin Oberweger, Gabe Aluisy, Barbara Grassey, Rhonda Robinson and Anthony Kovic for your unconditional support in creating this work.

Special thanks to The Wealth Building Annex, Tampa Bay Business Owners, Edison Council, Florida Podcasters Association, Podfest Multimedia Expo, 1 Million Cups and Entrepreneurs Organization.

For my wife, Katie and daughters, Sedona & Savannah. To Nonny and Poppy, Yia Yia and Papou: I love you all for all the love and support you've given me as you've seen me start ugly over and over again!

Start Ugly is a parable about dealing with change.

"The world as we have created it is a process of our thinking. It cannot be changed without changing our thinking."

— Albert Einstein

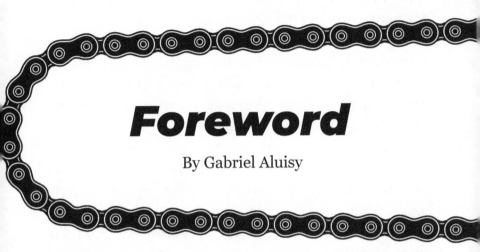

Foreword

By Gabriel Aluisy

The lesson in this book just might change your life. It surely changed mine. In fact, if Chris hadn't pushed me along the way, I'd likely be a lot less happy and certainly less fulfilled. I would have probably given up years ago or, worse yet, never tried.

Change is scary. Most of us are too afraid to step into a new opportunity, innovate or simply change our habits because we're afraid of failure. That fear is built into our DNA. It's normal to feel it. In fact, it would be strange if you didn't. I know I have - many times. Heck, I still do!

About 5 years ago, Chris asked me to present at one of his business symposiums. I had never spoken to an audience for any length of time and I was deathly afraid of public speaking.

I told Chris I didn't think I had it in me. He knew my content however, and he told me it was so valuable that folks would still embrace the message even if my performance was lacking.

I knew public speaking was the way to get my message out to more folks, build my business and help others. Still mortified, I decided to team up with a co-presenter. It was the only way I could do it!

Over the next few weeks I prepared my content. I also prepared myself. My mirror became my audience. I learned what a power-pose was. I practiced the "calming breath" that I had learned when my wife had our first child to ease my anxiety. Finally, the day came and I felt as prepared as I could be.

There were a few speakers that morning and I studied how smoothly they spoke and carried themselves. I admired that. I told myself over and over in my head that I could do it.

"Just relax," I told myself. I started to feel relatively confident.

That quickly changed. Between sessions as I was getting mic'd up by the sound guy I saw the camera. I looked at the seats. Suddenly I felt very warm. My mouth dried up. I started to sweat.

I thought to myself, "Oh no, no, no, no. Breathe, just breathe."

I looked at my co-presenter. She was just as nervous as me and she muttered something to that effect which I barely processed because my body was going into fight or flight mode.

Before I could have an all out panic attack our names were called and we were walking up to the stage. Like it or not, this was happening. My co-presenter started and a few minutes later it was my turn. I barely got the words out. I stumbled multiple times. I completely bombed.

Or so I thought. The thing is, my content was good. In fact, people came up to me afterwards telling me how much they enjoyed it. A friendly guy named Scott told me how much he agreed with my talking points. Chris had been right!

I just needed to start. I could refine it later, but I needed to start.

Chris did it again about a year later. He pulled me aside at a networking event he was running and told me I really needed to consider starting a podcast.

"I don't think so, Chris," I told him. "I hate the sound of my voice, I don't think folks will like it either."

"Podcasting is going to be big," he told me. "You need to get in now while the time is right."

He harped on me for the better part of a year. All the while I made up a lot of excuses about not wanting to figure out the technology, not having the time and how folks would hate my voice.

But I did want to keep speaking. I knew I had to get better at it too. Maybe a podcast would help me find my voice, I thought.

"Just start ugly," Chris kept telling me. "If it's not good, you don't have to put it out."

Ok I thought. I'll give it a shot. Maybe it will help me become a better public speaker. Maybe it will help me to cut out my, "ums."

So I bought a microphone. Being nervous and anxious I wrote out everything I needed to say. Wing it? No way! I scripted out every word.

I hit record and got about four words in before I stumbled. It took me about 25 takes, reading and rereading every line, to get my first 8 minute podcast recorded. It took another 3 hours to edit it!

I released 3 episodes to start. But would anyone really want to listen? Would anyone like what they heard if they did?

I quickly found out folks liked it. I also had a number of people tell me how much they liked my voice.

"It's so soothing and real" one nice lady told me.

I told her, "Thank you so much," but I thought to myself, "Soothing? My voice? Soothing? Real? Yeah, maybe that part."

After 20 episodes or so I started to feel more comfortable. I got better and finally relaxed. I found my voice. Today you can't shut me up in front of a mic.

The Private Club Radio Show has now reached tens of thousands of private club professionals around the world. It's the most-listened to podcast on the business of private golf and country clubs. It established me as one of the top experts in the field.

It's led to speaking engagements all over the world - I've spoken on four continents now. It took practice, lots of practice, but now I can finally say that I'm pretty damn good.

It's led to interviews in the New York Times and other top publications. It's led to bestselling books. In fact, my books are in 1 out of every 2 clubs in the United States.

It also led to a new fear - the fear of success. The fear of success is just as real as the fear of failure and it can be just as crippling. You might hear the term, "imposter syndrome" used to describe it. It's when you feel like you got lucky, like you didn't deserve it or this is going to be temporary.

That's something you might feel if you do something remarkable and have success you felt was unexpected. It's a lie and you need to recognize it as such. Because if you did it, *you* did it. You didn't get lucky. You won.

If I'm being honest, I still struggle with it occasionally. But with more and more success, and a bit of time, it fades.

Chris was right all along. I just needed to start ugly. You do too.

Most folks don't try because they're afraid to fail. They're paralyzed by it. But some ideas just need to be brought to life. And you are the person that needs to do it. You are their creator. Your ideas need you. Don't let them down.

Godspeed.

Table of Contents

Introduction: Why Start UGLY?

In my late twenties, I went through a period where money and accomplishments left me feeling unfulfilled. So, I took six months off to figure out how I wanted to spend the rest of my life.

I used that time to ask myself some foundational questions:

What did I want my life to be?

How did I want to live it?

What would motivate me to contribute to it?

I knew I wanted to help other people, but how? In what realm?

I chose business and the realm of community. During that time, I'd take walks at sunset on Davis Island in Tampa, Florida and envision the community I would bring together and what it would look like. Little did I know what I was about to do was "Start Ugly." *Really* ugly.

I gathered all my friends and business contacts, told them about this community of business owners I wanted to create, and invited them out to my first ever event.

I must have succeeded at the promotions side of things because ninety-nine people showed up to my first ever live event! Mind you, I knew nothing about putting on live events, but a friend of mine, Mr. Diaz, offered up his American Legion Hall for $300, and I was off to the races.

This was in Tampa during our very hot summer season. As luck would have it, the air-conditioner broke down that day, and the place reeked of cigars from the Legionnaires who'd gotten together to play poker the night before. I had asked everyone to wear business professional attire to the meeting.

To say I started ugly is an understatement. I pitched an idea for a group created for business owners by business owners and prayed people would forgive me for dragging them into a hot sweaty legion hall in the middle of a south Florida summer.

I put out one-page flyers, inviting people to join at the Ambassador level or as charter VIP's. At the end of the event, the chairs were littered with the flyers people had left behind.

Discouraged, I collected the sheets and was about to throw them into the garbage when a friend stopped me. "Look," she said. "A bunch are filled out."

To my amazement, twenty people had joined, and the seeds were planted for what would become the largest group of business owners in the area, growing to more than three-hundred members over the next decade.

Quickly, I moved the organization to a hotel and later to a business club where I refined and perfected the craft of facilitating my professional communities. Had I not had the guts to start ugly I would not be where I am today, more than two thousand events later!

Since then, I have started numerous associations and worked with business people, executives, and creatives alike. I have been in the room with people teaching Lean Six Sigma, Agile and numerous professional methodologies. Yet when I tell a roomful of people there is nothing like Starting Ugly, they seem to grasp the concept instantly.

What is the foundational principle of Starting Ugly? Basically, you need to do some research and planning but then you need to put your ass on the line and take action! That's your Start Ugly moment.

You can't wait for perfection. Or to be perfectly organized. You can't wait for approval. You have to be thoughtful in creating a plan, but more than anything, you must BEGIN.

Recently, a relative told me they were thinking of brewing their own beer. My response: *stop thinking and start doing.*

But it cost more than he could afford, he said.

I told him to ask for money or the brewing setup for his birthday.

When I mentioned that he'd lost precious time thinking—and not doing, he confessed that he'd been considering brewing his own beer for eight years! How many days, weeks, months, years of time do we squander on things we could get done almost immediately?

To really drive the point home, I offered the Start Ugly Story I had crafted. It made him see things in a new light, just as it has for many people in my life.

After numerous requests from friends and family to write down the story, I took my own advice and slowly, yet steadily, used the "Start Ugly" philosophy to write the *Start Ugly* book.

My hope is you will share this book with anyone finding challenges in getting started or stuck in old ways of doing things. In this age where there are so many experts and so much information coming at us, it's easy to get bogged down in the desire for perfection. The idea of starting ugly, then, is more relevant than ever.

The Retreat

"Hello, Chris speaking."

"Hi, Chris. This is James Davis. I found your speaker page on the web and was wondering if you could talk to my group of entrepreneurs who are on a retreat about technology and the disruption of it."

"Absolutely. When and where?"

"This Monday. Three PM?"

"That's short notice, but I think we can make it happen!"

And we did.

After the class, the group was amazed at the opportunities in front of them! And then their fears started bubbling up through their questions.

"Chris, all of this is fine and dandy, but I can't find good employees."

"I've been getting ghosted by my own people. Have you ever heard of this happening?"

"Chris, how do I find the time?"

"I just don't have the bandwidth."

"I'm doing a-okay, but the competition is paying their employees more."

"The technology is great and all, but who's going to train my people to use it?"

And on and on.

That's when I shared with them this parable I created.

The Start UGLY Story

A t the turn of the twentieth century, one man stood alone in the lumber industry. His name was Gregory Sharp[1], a bonafide self-made man who stood six-feet-two-inches tall.

Gregory came from humble roots. His parents immigrated from Europe as laborers, and by the time Gregory was twelve years old both his parents had passed away from consumption (tuberculosis) related diseases and left him caring for his four younger siblings.

Growing up on Manhattan Island, working in lumber mills, Gregory worked seven days a week, fourteen hours a day, as a child laborer. From his struggles, and the struggles of those around him, he developed a vision that someday he would revolutionize the lumber industry into something that was unified and integrated, from the tools the lumberjacks used to the way they processed the wood in the mills.

He held a philosophy that was tried and true. When asked by people how he was going to open up his own lumber mill, he would answer, "perfect execution!"

He figured by executing perfectly, he would create so many efficiencies within the business that the leaner business model would provide greater profits faster than his peers, allowing him to constantly grow.

By chance, Gregory met a man by the name of Bernard[2] who took a liking to the sixteen-year-old young man who cared for his younger siblings and dreamed of better ways of doing things.

Bernard was a financier on Wall Street, and after listening to the passion in Gregory's voice, he agreed to invest in his concept of a lumber mill with a full time R&D lab and hours that gave workers time to build a life outside of work.

Bernard offered some key advice: "Perfect Execution is mission critical. It's a key ingredient to success. Another is to be willing to experiment with new innovations even though the start might feel and look ugly. Keep both in mind, and you're bound to prosper."

Shortly after Gregory opened his first lumber mill, he fell in love with a young lady, Sara, a genius with numbers who had worked in her father's accounting business. She fell head over heels for this man who wanted to build a business that took care of its employees and stayed on the cutting edge. Together they ran the Sharp Lumber Mill, always looking at better ways to harvest wood...*to deliver a superior product more efficiently.*

BE WILLING TO
EXPERIMENT WITH NEW
INNOVATIONS.

Sharpening the Axes

The thought at the time was that you just got bigger, stronger guys to swing those axes. But Gregory brought on assistants who he tasked with sharpening the axes. He and Sara set up a lab to test metals to see which would hold an edge better than others. They studied the way their best axe men swung their axes. What was their stance? What was the arc of the swing? Was it better to hit straight on or at an angle? Did the most productive axe men have a certain rhythm?

They conducted training days to teach their people how to swing an axe more efficiently, how to get the most from every swing without wearing themselves out. They gave their employees days off because they realized that a day of rest enabled the employees to be more productive.

Everybody wanted to be part of the company. It treated its workers well and was at the forefront of the industrial revolution.

Their key competitive advantage was their research and development lab, where they pioneered lighter and stronger metals to make their axes. They also created special dual blade axes for multiple uses out in the field, allowing for longer cutting time.

All the business newspapers of the day featured Gregory Sharp as a business maverick for integrating the lumber mill process from the trees to the mill to your door. Local business leaders sought his advice and local politicians pursued his endorsement.

When asked what made him so special, Gregory would reply, "Perfect Execution!"

"We measure twice before we cut," he would say. "We use the lightest metal alloys in our axes. We have a line of people out the door that want to work for us, and we pick the best of them for the Sharp Lumber Mill."

WE MEASURE TWICE
BEFORE WE CUT

A New Hire's Happy Accident

One day, a young man by the name of Jeff[3] ap-
peared for an interview. He had a boyish en-
ergy and contagious exuberance that reminded
Gregory of himself as a younger man.

Jeff came from a great home and went to an Ivy League
college to study engineering. He loved solving complex
problems with the simplest solutions.

During his interview, Gregory asked Jeff if he had ever
seen a lumber mill as efficient as his. Jeff replied that
once on a scientific expedition in the Amazon, he had
seen native tribesmen use the force of the Amazon river to navigate lumber down to other tribes. Intrigued,

Gregory hired the young man on the spot.

Jeff looked up to Gregory as a revolutionary who had changed the lumber industry and wanted to make him proud. One day while he was riding his bicycle into work, his chain came off, and Jeff skidded across a newly installed wooden telephone pole.

He looked down to find that the chain had made a mark against the pole, and a kernel of an idea took shape in Jeff's inquisitive brain. He asked himself, "what if I could take a bike chain, arm it with a set of teeth, and rotate it via some form of combustible engine?"

His first version almost set the entire R&D lab on fire.

His second version could cut into a piece of wood at least two-inches deep. At which time Gregory came by to see how he was progressing on a faster, lighter axe.

When Jeff demonstrated what he was working on, Gregory grew furious that his money was being spent on such a frivolous device. Gregory immediately instructed Jeff to go back to work on designing a lighter sharper axe.

A KERNEL OF AN
IDEA TOOK SHAPE...

Another Look

O ne morning, Sara Sharp stopped by the R&D lab, and Jeff demonstrated the bike chain saw. Seeing Jeff's passion for this new creation and believing in its potential, Sara decided to ask her husband to give Jeff more leeway and time with his new invention.

That night during dinner Sara asked, "Gregory what do you think of Jeffrey's new invention?"

"What self-respecting Lumberjack would swing a bicycle chain to cut down a tree?" Gregory asked. "We're axe men, and axes are our tools!"

Sara kindly noted that Gregory was not ready to listen and asked him to have his mentor and investor Bernard take a look.

Gregory agreed, and Bernard paid a visit to the lab where he found himself fascinated with this young man and his unwavering belief that his new creation represented the future of the lumber industry. Jeff also shared his ideas of sustainable logging along the Hudson River Valley and a way to use the waterways to transport lumber right into the mills on Manhattan island, just like he had seen in the Amazon.

WHAT SELF-RESPECTING LUMBERJACK WOULD SWING A BICYCLE CHAIN TO CUT DOWN A TREE?

Last Chance

Bernard went back to Gregory and told him the young man was onto something. But Gregory just grew angry that his two closest confidants couldn't see how much time and money Jeff was wasting. He could have easily developed a sharper, lighter, stronger axe in the time he spent trying to develop this foolish bike chain saw.

Instead of giving Jeff more time, Gregory stormed into the lab and told him he had one week to build an efficient model of the bike chain saw, or he'd be out of a

43

job.

When the day for the demonstration came, an exhausted Jeff began to use what he now dubbed "The Chainsaw." He began to cut right into a huge oak tree, but halfway through the saw started to vibrate and broke into pieces, nearly severing Jeff's hand!

Gregory had had enough. This young man knew nothing about executing perfectly. He'd squandered Gregory's money and time designing something that had no legs.

Being a kind and honest man, Gregory signed a paper giving the young man all legal rights to this waste of parts now called the chainsaw and offered Jeff two weeks' pay to figure out what he was going to do next. A generous gesture for the times.

THIS YOUNG MAN
KNEW NOTHING ABOUT
EXECUTING PERFECTLY.

The Lifeline

Not knowing what to do, Jeff went to Sara to thank her for believing in him and his invention. He asked for any referrals she might have.

"Go to Lafayette Park during lunch time tomorrow," she told him. "I'll have our friend Bernard come speak to you."

True to her word, Bernard sat waiting for Jeff in the park the next day.

"Would you like to pursue this creation any further?" Bernard asked.

"It would be a dream come true," Jeff told him.

So, Bernard funded Jeff's invention and within a short time they'd smoothed out all the kinks that plagued the chainsaw in its infancy.

Hearing that Bernard had backed Jeff, and feeling that it was conflict of interest, Gregory insisted that Bernard divest his shares back to the Sharp Lumber Mill. Bernard complied, making a pretty penny as the stock was at a record high.

Gregory professed to Bernard, "You'll lose every cent you plow into that contraption! It's doomed to fail!"

WITHIN A SHORT TIME THEY'D SMOOTHED OUT ALL THE KINKS THAT PLAGUED THE CHAINSAW IN ITS INFANCY.

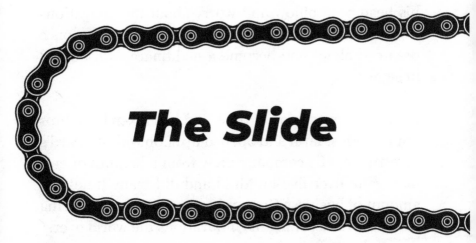

The Slide

By refusing to heed to the innovation taking place around him, Gregory started to experience things he had never experienced before. Key employees left for other firms. Payroll was a struggle each and every month.

Sara, being the amazing CFO she was, ran projections and told Gregory, "If we keep running the business the way we are we'll be "Perfectly Executing" ourselves and our employees out of a company!"

Over time, Gregory went from hiring men for a booming business to plateauing in growth. The papers no longer wrote articles about him, and politicians stopped coming by for his endorsement. His remaining employees' morale sank with the company's fortunes. Many of the benefits Gregory offered had to be cut in order to keep everyone employed.

Sleep became a tortured exercise where he would lay his head on a pillow and worry about the obligations he had to meet the next day. The business he once dreamed about had become a nightmare with no end in sight.

Over the same period of time, Jeff had taken his lumps but never lost faith and opened up shop with Bernard's investment. His company grew from a handful of employees to over five-hundred and did many times the amount of business Gregory's ever did, manufacturing chainsaws and selling his innovations the world over.

THE BUSINESS HE ONCE DREAMED ABOUT HAD BECOME A NIGHTMARE WITH NO END IN SIGHT.

Looking for a Sign

O ne bitter-cold winter night, feeling the pressure of letting down his employees, wife, children, and investors, Gregory locked his doors and went for a long walk along the Hudson River.

For the first time in his life he had lost his sense of self. He was stuck, rudderless, with no idea where to turn for help. Gregory was a strong and proud man yet tears of desperation streamed down his face. He was about to lose everything for which he'd worked so hard.

As Gregory walked along the Hudson River, he found himself blinded by a brightly lit sign from a new manufacturing plant he recognized as Jeff's. Seeing this as

both a literal and figurative sign, Gregory dried his eyes
and ran toward it.

Gregory had let his beard grow long, and due to the
stress had gained quite a bit of weight, making him almost unrecognizable to those who'd known him just
a few short years earlier. Security, thinking he was a
homeless man, denied him entry, but Gregory dashed
around their checkpoint and ran right into Jeff's office.

Security guards chased after him, grabbing Gregory
and trying to drag him out. But when Jeff looked into
the strange man's eyes, he realized it was his former
boss, Mr. Sharp, a man he still greatly admired. He
asked the men to leave him at once and invited Gregory
to have a seat at the chair in front of his desk.

FOR THE FIRST TIME
IN HIS LIFE HE HAD
LOST HIS
SENSE OF SELF.

The Realization

"What happened to you?" Jeff asked.

In a panic, Gregory began to sputter:

"How did you grow so fast?"

"How is this possible?"

"I did everything right!"

"I took care of my employees!"

"I made sure they had benefits! A living wage! Honest hours!"

59

"I pioneered the five day work week!"

"This is not fair!"

"The newspapers loved me, and business leaders all over the world sought out my advice. Politicians used me as the poster boy for innovation and execution."

"What did I do wrong, Jeff? What? *I executed everything perfectly!*"

Feeling pain for his old employer, Jeff leaned in and looked Gregory directly in the eyes and asked, "do you really want to know?"

Greg having lost all sense of EGO and pride yelled out:

"Yes, Jeff. I really want to know!!!"

"You fell so in love with your motto of 'Perfect Execution,' that you forgot to "Start Ugly" and innovate the way you once did when you first began."

For the first time in a long time Gregory was speechless. Jeff's words punched him right in the gut.

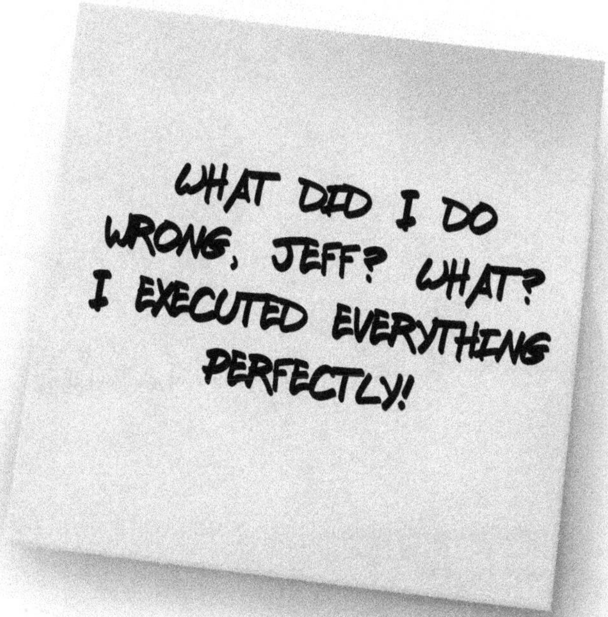
WHAT DID I DO
WRONG, JEFF? WHAT?
I EXECUTED EVERYTHING
PERFECTLY!

START
UGLY
START
UGLY
START
UGLY
START
UGLY
START
UGLY
START
UGLY

Time to Start UGLY

"Look around my office," Jeff continued. "What motto do you see?"

Two words were emblazoned on signs all around the office.

"Start Ugly," Gregory murmured. Over and over again, those words swam before him.

"Yes!" Jeff exclaimed. "Start Ugly! Gregory, this is the gift you gave me when you fired me from your organization. I never forgot that lesson, and I remind myself every day that you cannot execute anything perfectly if you are unwilling to start ugly again and again."

"You're right," said Gregory. "I forgot. I didn't want to change. I didn't want to believe I had to start ugly over and over again to keep growing."

Something in him sparked back to life at the realization. He felt hope for the first time in a while. "Jeff," he said. "Can I help you here?"

"It's so funny you asked," said Jeff. "Because we're in need of a local mill to test out our most innovative equipment and help make it better. I can't think of a better partner than Sharp Lumber Mill."

That night, Gregory went home, and for the first time in a long time was able to sleep, knowing there was a future to live into for his business and family.

The next day he sat down with Sara and created a plan to rebuild and retool his lumber mill, making it the most cutting edge and efficient facility in the country. He was **starting ugly** and willing to **execute perfectly** within a new vision for his entire industry.

HE HAD A FUTURE TO LIVE INTO

Words to Live By

Humbled, Gregory went back to Bernard and apologized for forgetting the words of advice his mentor had once given him:

*"**Perfect Execution** is mission critical. It's a key ingredient to success.*

*Another is to be willing to experiment with new innovations even though the **start** might feel and look **ugly**.*

Keep both in mind, and you're bound to have lasting success."

Beliefs Can Imprison Us

Many of you have heard or read the parable below before, but it serves as a powerful reminder of the Start Ugly principles.

***

A terrible storm came into a town, and local officials sent out an emergency warning that the riverbanks would soon overflow and flood the nearby homes. They ordered everyone in the town to evacuate immediately. A faithful preacher heard the warning and decided to stay, saying to himself, "I will trust God and if I am in danger, God will send a divine miracle to save me."

The neighbors came by his house. "We're leaving," they said. "There's room for you in our car. Please come with us."

But the preacher declined. "I have faith that God will save me."

The floodwaters rose, pouring water into his living room, and the man had to retreat to the second floor. A police motorboat came by and saw him at the window. "We will come up and rescue you!" they shouted. But the preacher waved them off. "Use your time to save someone else! I have faith that God will save me!" The flood waters rose higher and higher, forcing the man to climb up onto his roof.

A helicopter spotted him and dropped a rope ladder. Down came a rescue officer who pleaded with the preacher. "Grab my hand, and I'll pull you up!"

The preacher *still* refused, folding his arms across his chest. "No, thank you! God will save me!"

Shortly after, the powerful waters destroyed the house, sweeping the preacher away and drowning him.

In Heaven, the preacher stood before God and asked, "I put all of my faith in You. Why didn't You save me?" Gently, God replied, "Son, I sent you a warning. I sent you a car. I sent you a motorboat. I sent you a helicopter. What more did you want?"

If you recall Gregory had three warnings:

1. There was Jeff himself;

2. His wife Sara told him to give it a second chance;

3 .Finally, his investor Bernard told him to give it another look.

The main point of this very powerful parable is that our beliefs can imprison us, making us blind to opportunity when it comes our way. The solutions may not be the ones we think we need, but stubbornness—and a reluctance to change—leads to negative outcomes.

More times than not, the answers are right in front of us, if we keep our eyes open and accept success when it's offered.

The True Power of Starting UGLY

O ne of my favorite speakers, Nido Quibein, loves to say, *"The only human being that welcomes change is a baby in a wet diaper."*

As we get older, we forget that in our first two years we were learning constantly, enduring the bumps and bruises along the way.

Starting Ugly is a fundamental truth for all of us, whether we're babies learning to turn over, sit up, crawl, walk and run or adults looking to embrace a new trade, new software, new workout, or new diet.

Some surgeon friends have challenged me, saying that, for them, starting ugly might risk another person's life! They must execute perfectly.

True, of course, but I like to ask this question: "Did someone have to start ugly to make the procedure you do possible?" The answer is almost always "yes."

There is a time to execute perfectly and a time to start ugly. Often, successful entrepreneurs resist starting ugly again for fear of disrupting their status quo. But, as with Gregory in our parable, that resistance leads not to continued success but to stagnation and failure.

Perfect execution is absolutely needed in order to get better at what you do, once you've begun. However, in the age of innovation, starting ugly is crucial to success. In our ever-evolving world, change comes at a faster pace than ever before, and we have to be ready for it.

This fundamental rule applies to creatives as much as it applies to business people. Creatives who rewrite and rework their pieces need to set a date, release what they have, and go from there. You can always create something but finishing and putting it out into the world is as important as the process of creation.

One fundamental fact of success, for business people and creatives alike, is that your work will be criticized. There's no getting around it. Unless you refuse to try new things, at some point you'll have to offer your new vision to an audience.

Starting ugly means inviting criticism. Celebrate that! Now, your creations are worth people's time and attention. Now, you have something to show for yourself, whether or not everyone else admires your vision. Whenever possible, separate the valuable critiques from the unhelpful ones and use the former to get better at what you do.

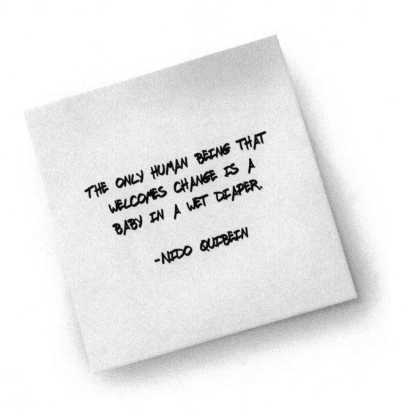

THE ONLY HUMAN BEING THAT
WELCOMES CHANGE IS A
BABY IN A WET DIAPER.

-NIDO QUBEIN

The Start UGLY Process

It's important to note that Start Ugly doesn't mean starting without thought or planning. It just means that you need to take action sooner rather than later, rather than agonizing over small details or expecting to be perfectly primed for success.

Here are the principles to help you lay a solid foundation for Start Ugly success:

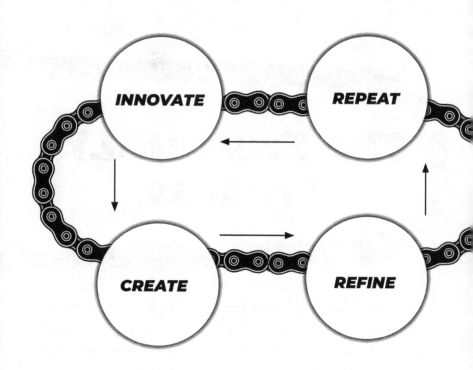

(1) Identify an opportunity or new way of doing things.

(2) Research what you're getting into and set a time limit for that research. Don't allow yourself to get bogged down trying to prepare for every eventuality.

(3) Create a minimal viable "thing," whatever that is, something you're proud to share with the world. Don't get stuck on perfection.

(4) Commit to a launch date. To make it real, make it public by telling people.

(5) Start Ugly and launch!

(6) Set check-in dates to assess:

A. If you determine you don't like what you started, STOP. Congrats! You don't have to think about it anymore.

B. If you love what you're doing, decide what your endeavor will become (new business, new division, side hustle, hobby, etc.). Set milestones accordingly.

(7) Create systems and work toward perfect execution.

**And now...Go back to Step 1
and Start Ugly again** ☺

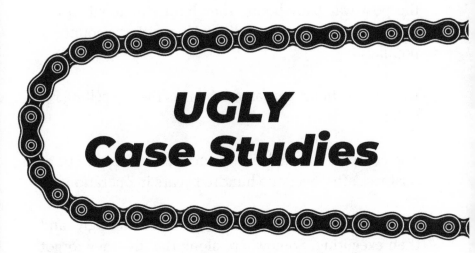

UGLY Case Studies

I n 1886, a small catalog company started selling watches and jewelry, distributing products directly to people's doors.

This company was at the forefront of starting ugly, and as the innovators of the time, they reaped tremendous benefits. They grew rapidly and over the next few years they created the Holiday Wish Book for people looking to shop during the holiday season.

In 1925, they created stores in the largest cities in the country and bought a radio station to help them get the word out about their stores and products.

In 1945, they hit one billion dollars in sales. They created their own signature lines of appliances, tools and car batteries.

In 1953, they introduced their own credit card. During the post-war baby boom, they built stores out in the emerging suburbs, expanding along with the country's population.

In 1991, Walmart surpassed them as the top selling retailer.

The company was SEARS. In 2018, Sears went out of business after over one hundred years in operation.

The very DNA of Sears was built on "Starting Ugly" and then executing. Somewhere along the line they forgot about all the innovations that led to their massive success. They just kept executing on the same plan they'd created decades prior.

When the internet was in its infancy, Sears was perfectly positioned to go back to its roots in a different medium. They could have become a robust online catalog company, beating Amazon to market.

Unfortunately, the executives at the helm had forgotten what made the company special, and that cost them their business.

***

In his book GOOD TO GREAT, one of the companies Jim Collins features is Circuit City. The book was released on October 16, 2001. Circuit City shut its doors on November 8, 2008.

Founded by Samuel S. Wurtzel in 1949, Circuit City sold emerging technologies at the time, like the television set.

Its growth trajectory was spotty, and in the early 1970's, it almost went under, due to its strategy of buying up other mom and pop retailers and rolling them into the existing culture.

After writing off the losses and moving on, son Alan Wurtzel assumed the role of CEO from 1972 through 1986, growing the company to one billion in sales and creating a powerful track record for growth.

When Alan handed over the reins to his successor, his strategy remained intact, allowing Circuit City to grow to ten billion in sales. But in his book, GOOD TO GREAT TO GONE, author Wurtzel relates that the company lost its way by never making adjustments to its original strategies.

Unlike its competitors, like Best Buy, they stayed on a fixed course, and this inability or unwillingness to start ugly again led to the demise of a company considered great enough to be featured in a book about success only seven years earlier. They were frozen in an outdated model, perfectly executing themselves out of business.

***

Jerry Seinfeld is arguably one of the most successful standup comedians of all time. When asked why he named his show Seinfeld he said, "We weren't sure it would last, but I hoped the show title would at least give my standup gigs more recognition so I could sell bigger venues."

Jerry made a show about nothing into everything! After nine seasons at the top, he decided to call it quits. The network offered him anything he wanted. New shows. A production deal. More money. He turned it all down and decided to start ugly again.

After nine years away from standup, he built new routines. He's said that he didn't want to become what everyone wanted him to become. He just wanted to be happy.

Then for fun he started "Comedians in Cars Getting Coffee," an internet show that features Jerry driving around and talking to comedian friends, on the road and over coffee.

When asked why he didn't take it to TV he said, "It feels kind of backward. I'm in everyone's phone. Why do I want to restrict it to a network?"

Time after time, Jerry Seinfeld has demonstrated what it means to start ugly while keeping his creative curiosity and perfect execution at the forefront of everything he does.

***

In 2013, I featured a friend of mine at a local workshop on the topic of podcasting. The topic got me so excited that I went home to share what I learned with my wife. She said she wanted to start a podcast.

At the time we were producing over 150 live events a year, and our business consultant recommended that only one of us start a podcast as the business needed our full attention. That led to our first podcast-related fight...I mean discussion!

Since Katie already had a niche, I chose to be her marketing manager while she pumped out the content for her podcast Biz Women Rock. Five years in, Katie had built a successful consulting business, helping women all over the world.

At first, Katie didn't really know how to structure her consulting practice, but by offering complimentary sessions to her listeners, she found she was really good at it and learned the best methods for helping women entrepreneurs. Within short order, Katie had a stable of paying clients.

Since that time, Katie and I have welcomed two beauti-ful little girls, Sedona and Savannah, into our lives. The demands of motherhood prompted Katie to consider what else she could do that would serve her calling and allow her more hours with our girls.

She chose to pivot and start ugly again, producing The Women's Meditation Network. What did Katie know about producing mediations? Nothing, other than she loved listening to them. What she truly loved was an opportunity to create something that spoke to women's subconscious every day, supporting them so they could achieve greater success and greater inner peace.

As she was getting her new podcast together, I sug-gested that Katie listen to all the mediations out there to determine what she liked and didn't like and, most importantly, how she could add more value for the lis-tener.

In doing so, Katie discovered her unique ingredient. She would state the intention prior to starting the guid-ed meditation. As simple as that. Fast forward a year, and Katie now has tens of thousands of listeners and advertisers lined up to sponsor her show.

Her first offerings were bumpy, but her commitment to improving and executing each and every episode has really helped her create truly special meditations wom-en embrace.

If Katie feared starting ugly, she'd never have become a bolstering voice for so many women the world over—twice! My girls and I are super proud to have such an amazing force for change in our lives.

***

When the Tampa Bay Business Owners was formed in June of 2008, I faced an unanticipated challenge. All my original members made a living in real estate. This was during the heart of the real estate bust in Florida!

In February of 2009, I formed eMarketing Groups, a meetup system open to the public to learn about an emerging field called "social media." I hosted it on a newer site called Meetup.com. I didn't know where I would find my educators. I barely knew how to use Meetup and posted the wrong address the first time I ever held a meeting.

By starting this group, I unknowingly created a source of potential members for the Tampa Bay Business Owners, one that included people in other fields than real estate.

The eMarketing Groups system grew to encompass the entire Tampa Bay area and held four weekly meetups at its peak. Over time we added social media accounts on several platforms and also created an online group for our members to continue the dialog within a group setting.

In 2015, I created a small conference on the emerging medium of podcasting. In 2016, I sold Tampa Bay Business Owners and started ugly, building a conference-based business in the field of podcasting. Its lead offering, Podfest Expo, has quickly become one of the top conferences for podcasting, with its own tradeshow and educational tracks.

In starting ugly, we accept that nothing is perfect its first time out. We commit that we will move through the fear and learn from our starts and commit to improving all along the way.

More From Chris

When I first wrote this book and sent it to friends who are editors and writing pros, the feedback was...well, not pretty. Early on in the process, I received this comment: "First, please know that I love you. But this is not good. On the plus side, you have that "starting ugly" thing down, which gives you something to work with!"

Though the comment stung, I knew it was true, and I used it to motivate me to do better. I started ugly, but I didn't want the book to stay that way. So, I dug in and chiseled out the work you're reading today. It was ugly yet rewarding to create.

Another friend, Gabe Aluisy, pushed me along the way by actually planning a book launch party! He got so tired of me saying, "Yeah, I'm going to write that story down and publish the book" that he forced the issue. Unbeknownst to me, he posted on Facebook that I was publishing my book, set a date, and then invited people to attend the launch!

Gabriel Aluisy
April 22 ·

Congrats to Chris Krimitsos who is releasing his book on August 8th! Let me know if you want to invite to the party.

You, Shawn Yesner, John Largent and 40 others   26 Comments

👍 Like   💬 Comment   ↪ Share

Quite honestly, I truly appreciated this. Gabe bought into the Start Ugly philosophy even as I faltered.

This book is a tool to help you and those around you understand it's okay to start ugly as long as you're willing to grow and adjust after taking that important first step of starting. Of course, it's not Start Ugly, Stay Ugly. The goal is to start ugly, improve, and then execute perfectly. And when needed, know that you may have to start ugly all over again.

Keep a copy of this book on your bookshelves or desk so the words of START UGLY stare back at you, reminding yourself that excuses are just that and that you don't have to be perfect to start.

Starting Ugly can lead to beautiful things!

Respectfully, Chris Krimitsos

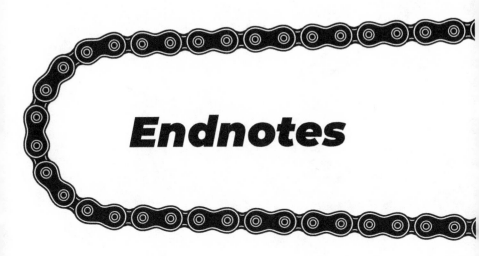

Endnotes

[1]Gregory represents Borders CEO Gregory Josefowicz, whose reluctance to start ugly in the author's opinion contributed to the company's demise.

[2]Bernard is an homage to the Lone Wolf of Wall Street, Bernard Baruch who--at the turn of the century--would hold court on a park bench in Lafayette park NYC. He was the original Warren Buffet way before Warren buffet.

[3]Jeff represents Amazon CEO, Jeff Bezos whose willingness to grow and adapt has propelled his company to unprecedented heights.

#START *UGLY*

About the Author

Chris Krimitsos is a father, husband, community builder and ever-evolving innovator. He loves people and their stories and has leveraged his gifts of connecting others to build communities around entrepreneurship, podcasting, and multimedia.

Chris was profoundly affected at 16 years of age when he watched his father loose a restaurant he had bought with sweat equity and eventually put the keys in for the last time giving it back to the bank. He vowed then that he would make it his mission to help business owners the world over to avoid that terrible fate.

Start Ugly is an extension of that promise and a story that can be understood by all who read it.

To Learn more about Chris visit his Website at ChrisKrimitsos.com

If you've made it this far in the book, I have one really big favor to ask of you: think of one thing you've been wanting to start and head to whatever social media platform you use and declare that you are ready to #StartUgly on whatever it is you have been delaying. Declare it. Use the hashtag #startugly. And tag me @ ChrisKrimitsos. Or send me a private message on any of those platforms. Seriously. I'm in your corner and excited to hear what you were able to accomplish by starting ugly!

Respectfully, Chris Krimitsos

Notes

Notes

Notes

CPSIA information can be obtained
at www.ICGtesting.com
Printed in the USA
BVHW031659270520
580336BV00004B/256